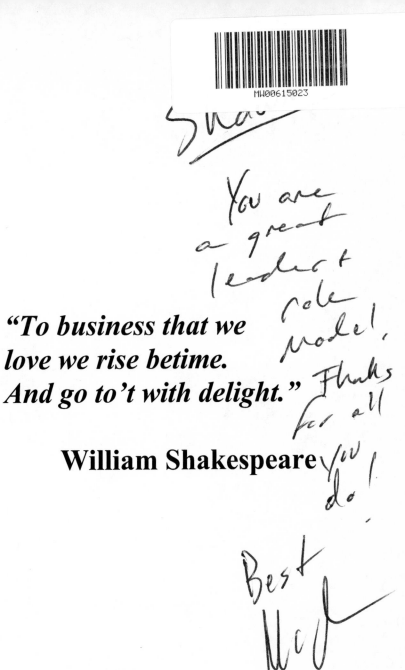

"To business that we love we rise betime. And go to't with delight."

William Shakespeare

MANANGING
for High Performance

by Gene C. Mage

To order additional copies of *Managing for High Performance,* complete the order form found on page 85 or visit www.makingitwork.com.

For information on Making it Work™ products and services call 1-866-290-1404 or visit www.makingitwork.com

Making it Work ™
459 Belwood Drive
Horseheads, NY 14845
866-290-1404

Printed in the United States of America
ISBN: 1-59196-072-X

9 781591 960720

Published by Making it Work™ Publications, Keynotes & Seminars
Printed in USA

A Word to the Reader

There are no **quick fixes** in this world. Reading this book will spark your imagination, inspire you to dig deeper, and motivate you to take action. In order to experience these benefits, may I suggest the following steps?

✔ Reading this book will stimulate **creative ideas** for your own organization. Capture these as you go in the **ideas** page at the end of each chapter.

✔ Reading this book will inspire you to **dig deeper**. Select resources from the **recommended reading** list on page 79 for more in-depth material on the topics you find particularly interesting.

✔ Reading this book will motivate you to act on issues in your own organization. Capture your specific **action items** as you go in the **ideas** page at the end of each chapter.

After reading this book, please order copies for your colleagues who would benefit from these ideas.

Contents

Chapter 1:   Earning the Right to Manage 7

Chapter 2:   Envisioning a Positive Work
Environment 23

Chapter 3:   Setting Conditions 31

Chapter 4:   Measuring Performance 39

Chapter 5:   Providing Consequences 45

Chapter 6:   Creating Your Performance
Management System 59

Chapter 7:   Deploying Your Performance
Management System 73

Recommended Reading List 79

About the Author 80

Chapter 1

Earning the Right to Manage

*The essence of **good management** is letting people know what you expect, inspecting what is done, and supporting those things that are done well.*

> --Zig Ziglar

*Great managers hold people accountable for **clearly agreed upon standards**, not unspoken expectations.*

> --Gene C. Mage

The Purpose of *Managing for High Performance*

Pity the manager, so misunderstood. Are managers bosses? Are managers owners? Or, as many employees believe, are they the dimwitted "pointy haired boss" exemplified in Scott Adam's Dilbert© comic strip?

What exactly is management anyway? What does effective management look like, and why is it so rare?

Why are workplaces with great managers so much more fun, positive, and motivating places to work?

More importantly, how can ordinary managers do the things that transform an ordinary organization into a great place to work?

I wrote **Managing for High Performance** to answer these questions. Reading this book will equip you, the manager, with a critical set of tools for getting high performance from your employees and superior results from your organization.

After studying management practices at some of the world's leading companies over the past five years, and personally deploying management training for one of America's most admired companies, I have identified a small set of core principles that will also work for you. These are foundational people-management principles that have been tested with executives, employees, and entrepreneurs. Put into practice, these principles transform the work of managing people from a fearful and frustrating duty to an exciting and rewarding privilege.

So if you or someone close to you would really like to put the fun back into the work of management, join me for the next few minutes as we discover *Managing for High Performance.*

The Manager's Job

So just what is your job as a manager? A manager is an individual who *takes responsibility* for the performance of other people.

The manager usually does not own the business, but is hired by the owners to get results. The manager practices *stewardship*, taking care of something that belongs to someone else.

> *The manager practices **stewardship**, taking care of something that belongs to someone else.*

The owners set expectations and demand that the manager perform to mutually agreed-upon standards. Those performance measures might be financial, such as revenues, gross margins, and earnings per share. Those performance measures might be less tangible, such as creating a certain image for the firm among customers and investors. But regardless of the metrics, the job of the manager is to deliver results to the owner.

To deliver those results, you as the manager have a set of levers you can pull. These levers are the tools in the manager's toolbox. You may hire employees who possess the background and personal traits to get results. You might invest capital in research, equipment, and acquisitions. You could vary the marketing mix, optimizing the product assortment, distribution channels, advertising campaign, and pricing strategy. But you must use every resource available to you to get results for the owners.

Importantly, virtually every civilized society demands that managers get those results using ethical practices. Those ethical guidelines may or may not be legally required, but are generally agreed upon statements about conduct. The most crucial of these ethical guardrails are **integrity, honesty, and fairness**. You can stop someone on the street of any city, from Boston to Bombay, and get quick agreement around basic, gut- level standards of right and wrong.

> *The most crucial of these ethical guardrails are **integrity, honesty, and fairness**.*

While you might get a certain amount of work done yourself, or even champion several high profile initiatives, you cannot do all the actual work required to get positive results. You must, first and foremost, set the conditions for individual employees to do their work. You must set clear expectations, provide resources, and eliminate barriers. You must provide the consequences that reinforce good results and helpful behaviors, and penalize poor results and counter-productive behaviors.

The Management Challenge

Unfortunately, too many managers are uncomfortable at best, and at worst clumsy, at managing the conditions and consequences which lead to organizational performance. When the individuals in an organization do not perform to high standards, the business results inevitably fall short. If the manager cannot coax high performance out of the talent in his care, his business will under-perform the competition.

Underperforming businesses are characterized by a long list of sub-standard outcomes, but here are a few of the most visible:

1. High employee turnover
2. Low employee morale
3. Missed financial targets
4. Repeated downsizing
5. Cost reduction focus
6. Acquisition driven growth
7. Incoherent and/or inconsistent strategic decisions
8. Hope in a heroic "savior" CEO
9. Hope in a world-beating new product

Do you recognize any of those symptoms? As W. B. Yeats wrote, "Though the leaves are many, the root is one…" All of these symptoms can be traced, in one form or another, to **poor management practices**. Organizations often spend decades trying to treat each of these symptoms while failing to address the root cause. Various programs putting salve on the wounds follow one after another, while employees become ever more cynical about the organization. After a while, people no longer trust that the management knows what they are doing.

Creating a Great Organization

I think anybody would like to join an organization that has a fun work environment and gets superior results. Interestingly, the organizations that put sound, ethical, and consistent processes in place to get good results, are often the most fun places to be. Why? Because **people like to work where they know what is expected** and have a fighting chance to succeed.

So in your organization, how will you know if you are winning? Your organization or department must set its own "standards" that define what good performance looks like. Part of the manager's job is to identify her personal list of metrics, based upon what her bosses, and ultimately the owners, demand.

So before you can begin to "manage" performance, you must decide what

> *People like to work where they know what is expected.*

"performance" looks like. You must have good agreements with your superiors about how results will be measured. You must then get clear in your own mind what you expect from your employees. Then you communicate those expectations to the people who will do the work.

A great manager holds people accountable for performing to **agreed-upon** standards. A great manager sets high standards, and expects people to reach those standards.

A tyrant, on the other hand, focuses on being in control. The tyrant has only vague, general notions about what he wants, and then punishes employees who fall short of his unspoken expectations. When the tyrant comes on the scene, high performing employees will head for the door.

An excellent manager knows she cannot hold people accountable for that which they have not agreed to do. You cannot follow up on that which you have not put into motion. Before you can provide consequences, you must first establish the conditions in which the employee can perform. Before you can manage, you must do your own homework, and earn the right to manage.

Employees understand that high performance ought to naturally result in praise, recognition, and tangible rewards, and

> *Before you can manage, you must do your own homework, and earn the right to manage.*

that poor performance results in corrective measures. The key, then, to a positive work environment, is a system that provides employees with three critical elements in a consistent and ethical manner:

✓ **Clear expectations** from the management as to what constitutes good job performance.

✓ **Conditions**, including resources, time, work processes, and equipment, that enable employees to do their job with excellence.

✓ **Consequences** that recognize and reward high performance, while correcting and eliminating poor performance.

Management Must be a System

An effective management system is a **series of conversations** between managers and employees during the year. Some of these conversations are spontaneous as part of the day-to-day work, while others are planned and structured to yield results. The system will also provide checklists to ensure thoroughness and forms for documenting what gets said.

These conversations occur in a definite sequence that enables you to set expectations, conditions, and consequences in a fair and supportive way. In the following chapters, you will read about each element of a sound performance management system.

Tools are Not Enough

Lots of organizations have systems for managing performance, but few can truly say that these systems are consistently embraced and followed by managers and employees. A system will work only if management fully believes in the **guiding principles** that underlie effective management. Without a commitment to this core set of ethical standards, the words of managing performance become nothing more than a collection of manipulative techniques.

Summary: Guiding Principles for Managing Performance

We believe that:

1. You can only get high performance when people are held accountable for achieving **high standards**.

2. You can only hold people **accountable** if you first:

   a. Set clear **expectations** for what is expected;

   b. Gain **agreement** from the employee to meet those expectations;

   c. Set clear **measures** for what constitutes high performance;

   d. Provide the **conditions** that enable the employee to perform, such as tools, resources, and organization;

   e. Provide regular **feedback** on performance.

3. People given clear expectations and regular feedback on performance will **manage themselves.**

4. **High performance** must be recognized and rewarded.

5. **Poor performance** must be corrected.
   a. **Before** we correct an employee we must first evaluate whether we, as managers, have provided the conditions for that employee to succeed;   ·
   b. **If** we have set the conditions, provided feedback, and have allowed the employee time to respond, then we have the right to provide correction;
   c. **Poor performance** must not be tolerated indefinitely. Correcting a non-performing employee is a process that has a definite ending point, either in improvement to acceptable performance, or removal of the employee from the position.

Only when we embrace these core beliefs about effective management and put these beliefs into practice, do we have the "right" to manage others. **Have you earned the right to manage**? Take the following "pop quiz" and see how you did.

Self Test: Have I Earned the Right to Manage?

✓ Have I communicated clear expectations to every employee?

    o   Does each of my employees have a job description?

    o   Does each of my employees have an agreed-upon goal plan?

    o   Does each of my employees know how he/she will be measured?

✓ Have I measured their results and provided regular feedback?

    o   Have I established performance metrics?

    o   Have I established standards of performance?

    o   Have I set up regular times to discuss job performance?

✔ Have I established the conditions which will allow my employees to do excellent work?

> o Do my employees have the resources, equipment, space, and training to do their jobs?

> o Do my employees have the knowledge and skill to get the results I expect?

> o Do my employees have agreements with other departments who supply vital information or work components they will need to get the results I expect?

If you can answer an honest yes to each of these nine homework assignments, you have earned the right to manage.

If you have not put each of these principles into practice, you must do them first **before** you can hold others accountable for their job performance. The tools provided on the following pages will equip you to build a great place to work through your own effective and ethical people management practices. Let's get started!

Chapter 2

Envisioning a Positive Work Environment

Have you noticed how some work environments are incredibly energizing places to be, while others are more like a stagnant, toxic swamp?

When I walk through a place of business I can sense pretty quickly whether the office atmosphere is positive, neutral, or negative. I guarantee that if employees are not having fun, they are not doing their best work, and that particular business is not performing as well as it could. Nine times out of ten I find they will have no effective system for managing people.

What does a great work environment look like? According to a number of studies conducted on workplace satisfaction, there are some specific, observable characteristics of positive work environments. Here are nine that I believe are excellent indicators:

1. **Clear expectations.** One of the first questions I ask employers is, "Do each of your

> *I guarantee that if employees are not having fun, they are not doing their best work, and that particular business is not performing as well as it could.*

employees have a job description?" Nothing gets employees frustrated faster than trying to figure out the unspoken expectations of their manager. Only when there are clear agreements between workers and managers about job responsibilities, along with standards for performance, can managers hold employees accountable for results.

2. **Courtesy and respect.** While none of us would do business very long with an enterprise that treated us disrespectfully, I am continually amazed at how many managers feel they can get away with discourteous behavior towards employees. As Wal*Mart founder, Sam Walton,

observed, "If you take care of the people in the stores, they will take care of the customers in the same manner."

3. **Honest appreciation.** It has been said that people work for money, but they live for recognition. People will put up with all kinds of workplace hassles if someone comes along at the end of the day with a sincere "Thank you" for a job well done.

4. **Regular feedback.** While nobody enjoys hearing criticism, it is even worse to hear nothing from the boss. I once asked an employee to prepare a report on a topic she felt was important. I got busy and never gave her feedback. That employee got incredibly angry, imputing to me all sorts of nefarious motives. Always give employees feedback on their work.

5. **Meaningful work.** Everyone on the payroll in a successful organization does something every day that contributes to the goals of the enterprise.

Each employee, from the floor sweeper to the CEO, needs to understand how his job, no matter how menial, contributes to the success of the whole.

6. **Opportunities to grow.** Growing employees do better work. Managers must talk with employees about their goals, dreams, and career aspirations. The boss and employee, working together, can then craft a realistic career plan that describes the future jobs the employee would like to achieve, along with the skills and experiences the worker needs to qualify.

7. **Tangible rewards.** Employees are constantly watching the management to determine which behaviors work in the organization. They draw conclusions about what attitudes and behaviors the management values by observing who gets ahead and who gets rewarded. Management must reward excellent performers through spoken praise, monetary rewards, and career advancement. Importantly, employees need to

26

understand how the quality of their work will impact their pay.

8. **Management that listens.** Want to engender a sense of commitment to the company? Ask employees for their opinions, advice, and inputs into key decisions. Show that you understand what they have to say, act on it when appropriate, and share the credit with the one who made the suggestion.

9. **High standards of excellence.** Who wants to call their mom and say, "I just got a job at one of the more mediocre firms in the area?" People want to be part of a winning team. Set high expectations and hold people accountable. If management looks the other way when a worker consistently falls short of company standards, other employees will conclude that poor performance is "OK". If the non-performing employee cannot improve within a reasonable timeframe, help them move on to a more suitable job.

> *A climate survey only takes the temperature, but does nothing about changing the thermostat.*

Many organizations conduct "climate surveys" to assess the state of the work environment. These surveys can be valuable, but often do more harm than good. Why? Because the very act of doing the survey creates an expectation on the part of the organization that you are going to do something about the issues. A climate survey only takes the temperature, but does nothing about changing the thermostat.

The key to building a positive work environment is a commitment to take positive action on a few critical factors. I propose that the most powerful factors that influence job satisfaction are found, you guessed it, in the behaviors of the management. **You are the single most important factor in building a great place to work**.

If you have excellent systems for managing employee performance, employees will feel good about their workplace. Challenge yourself to create and deploy an excellent system for your own organization.

Ideas: My Vision of a Positive Workplace

Clear Expectations	
Courtesy and Respect	
Honest Appreciation	
Regular Feedback	
Meaningful Work	
Opportunities to Grow	
Tangible Rewards	
Management that Listens	
High Standards of Excellence	

Chapter 3

Setting Conditions

When you strip away all of the nuances, a manager really has only two levers to pull. She can set the conditions for success and provide consequences for results. But before she can even begin to think about consequences, she must make sure that she has set the pieces in place to allow the performer to do his job.

What conditions does the manager set? Here are eight crucial conditions for high performing employees:

1. **A clear assignment, context, scope, and boundaries.**

   The most important condition you can set that will determine the success or failure of the worker to deliver the desired results is a clear assignment of work. If you delegate responsibility for a result, you must clearly articulate exactly what the deliverable will be. To illustrate this principle, let's look at a case study in which the employee, Janet, a marketing assistant, is delegated a task from Michele, the sales manager. Let's peek in on their conversation.

Michele calls Janet into her office and hands her a note, which reads, "Janet will prepare a report of unusual order patterns in the customer database and communicate that to the department every Tuesday." Janet reads the note and appreciates the fact that the assignment is in writing. Now she has some questions to make sure she does an excellent job.

Janet needs to discuss scope and boundaries of the project so she knows what is in and what is out. Janet asks, "Will the report cover all customers and product lines, or sub-sets of the data?" Janet will want to get clear definition about what "unusual" means; perhaps it would be a plus or minus 20% deviation from the norm. Does the boss want the report in print, or transmitted electronically? Janet must be clear about what the assignment entails before she leaves the room. But importantly, many employees will not take the initiative to ask every question, so you as the manager must anticipate these questions and prepare detailed information before the meeting.

Additionally, Janet will want to understand the context of the assignment. "What will the data be used for?" she asks. "Why weekly? Why Tuesday?" If she has some background on why the task is important to the department, Janet might come up with an improved format, or a way to eliminate the report altogether through an automated system. If she does not know the root issue behind the request, all she can do is comply. If she understands the business result that the assignment is meant to impact, she can put her creative energy to work helping get the result.

2. **Required resources.** Using our sales report example, what will Janet need to prepare the

assignment? Michele offers to help Janet get access to certain databases. "You will need the locations and passwords for those databases," Michele notes. Perhaps Janet needs analytical software to do the analysis. Perhaps she needs presentation software to publish the reports. Michele and Janet brainstorm a list of every imaginable resource. This way Janet does not need to come back to the boss two or three times to ask for what she needs.

3. **Information.** In this example, the information may be the data in the database. But there may be other information that Janet would find helpful. Perhaps she could review other reports being done in the group to see what colleagues have learned doing similar tasks. Maybe she should look at what was done in previous years or in other departments. Someone across the street in another building may have already done all the hard work of building the analysis and reporting tool. Why waste time re-inventing the wheel? Perhaps another operating unit in the

organization, or even a customer, supplier, or competitor is using a best practice approach to solving this problem. Michele encourages Janet to seek out these information sources to get the best possible result, and allows a couple of days of extra time to enable Janet to do that pre-work.

4. **Knowledge.** Does Janet know how to do the analysis and reporting this assignment requires? Or does she need to be trained, or work under the tutelage of an experienced co-worker?

5. **Skill.** Does Janet have the software skills to do what needs to be done?

6. **Organizational linkages.** Who else in the organization will Janet need cooperation from in order to do the assignment? Will she be dependent upon a corporate IT department? Will she need the time of a co-worker? As the manager, Michele greases the skids and eliminates barriers, so that Janet can get what she

needs.

7. **Measures of success.** How will Michele know if Janet did a good job? What will be the criteria? Will it be accuracy? Timeliness? Usefulness? Janet and Michele agree together up front on the standards of performance, so Janet can aim for success.

> *How will Michele **know** if Janet did a good job?*

8. **Follow up and accountability**. What will be the process for holding Janet accountable for getting the task done? Will there be a review at the first due date? How often will Michele give Janet feedback on the quality of her work? Janet and Michele agree that they will review the first installment of the new report in two weeks. In addition, they talk about the consequences for results. For instance, Michele lets it be known that she considers hitting certain standards to be very important and that chronically falling short will have negative consequences on the

performance of the group.

She also talks about how exceeding the standards will help the group, and Janet, at performance review time.

Ideas: Setting Conditions for Success

Clarity of scope and deliverables	
Resources	
Information	
Knowledge	
Skills	
Linkages	
Measures of Success	
Follow Up and Accountability	

Chapter 4

Measuring Performance

A client of mine who implemented the principles contained within this book was faced with the challenge of putting together performance metrics for evaluating employees. He successfully solved the problem by using three steps that I think you will benefit from as you choose your own set of organizational performance metrics. Here are his three steps:

1. **Start by asking, "What behaviors drive my business?"**
   Establishing performance metrics for your business can be one of the most valuable exercises you can possibly undertake. To identify performance metrics, you step back and objectively observe what people do and how those behaviors impact business results.

In the case of my friend's business, his employees produce products used by medical professionals in the treatment of patients. So he first picked a business outcome he wanted to work on, sales productivity. He then asked, "What behaviors drive sales productivity?" Rather than do an exhaustive ground-up study, he decided to simply examine what one of his most productive employees was actually doing. In other words, he picked an **exemplar,** and looked at what behaviors the exemplar exemplified!

The exemplar spent an inordinate percentage of time talking to doctors and used his office time very prudently. When he delivered the medical devices to patients he did so with one or two office visits, rather than multiple visits to make small adjustments to the device. When he placed work orders to the fabrication center where the devices were built, the exemplar carefully filled out each box on the order form, eliminating errors, delays, and rework.

After this study, the manager chose three metrics: time spent with doctors, speed of delivery, and order accuracy. Each of these things could be measured by observing the actual behaviors of the performer.

> *Each of these things could be measured by **observing the actual behaviors** of the performer.*

He then had a conversation with each performer to talk about what their individual performance standard would be. For example, he would describe to each performer what the company average was for delivery speed, what excellent delivery speed was, and what the minimum standard was. The manager and performer then agreed upon the employee's target for delivery speed.

2. **Keep it simple**

You will notice that the manager of the medical device company example chose only three measures. There were no doubt dozens of other things he could have measured, but he chose the few that he felt most directly impacted business results.

3. **Use three categories of measurements**

    a. **Business outcomes**: Business outcomes are the results of behaviors. These include sales, profit margins, cost control, and employee turnover.

    b. **Job performance behaviors**: These are the behaviors that lead to the business results. These include time with clients, quality, accuracy, speed, number of calls, and the use of good management skills, for example.

    c. **Interpersonal behaviors**: These are the behaviors that influence the overall productivity of the organization. For our medical device company, it was important that workers communicated with one another in a courteous, respectful tone. It was important that they were patient with one another during rush times. Again, these are behaviors that the manager and other employees can observe.

Once performance metrics have been established, they can be translated into user-friendly checklists and forms to help managers and employees document their goals and evaluate performance. If this manager chose three critical metrics for each of the categories, the goal plan and evaluation form would have only nine metrics in total. I think this should be the maximum.

Have you ever seen performance appraisal instruments with dozens of questions about every nuance of employee behavior? Complex, lengthy survey instruments are used grudgingly at best and ignored at worst. Keep it simple!

Ideas: My Performance Metrics

Behavioral drivers in my business	
Key metrics: business outcomes	
Key metrics: behaviors	
Key metrics: interpersonal behaviors	

Chapter 5

Providing Consequences

If you have set clear expectations and provided regular feedback, you are in a position to provide consequences for employees' actions. And nothing you can do as a manager has greater impact on behavior than consequences. According to research on human behavior, the conditions you set to create good performance account for about 15% of what happens, while consequences that occur after the employee does something account for about 85% of what happens.

Why are consequences so powerful?

People formulate their beliefs about what is and is not acceptable behavior by watching what happens to people who behave. For example, if an employee is chronically late and never receives a reprimand from the supervisor he will assume that being late is "OK". Not only will he see that being late is "OK", but every other employee will observe that there was no consequence for the behavior and assume that it is "OK" for them too.

> *People **formulate their beliefs** about what is and is not acceptable behavior by **watching what happens** to people who behave.*

To get the performance you want you need to **establish and consistently provide consequences** for behaviors and results.

As the manager, you have three basic categories of consequences at your disposal:

1. **Rewards:** You need to compensate and promote those people who do excellent work. If poor performers are also rewarded, the benefit to the high performer is meaningless. If excellent performers are not rewarded, others will conclude that performance does not really matter to the management.

2. **Recognition:** You need to comment publicly and enthusiastically when someone does something well. It might be a certificate of recognition or just a "thank you", but as they say, "people work for money, but they LIVE for recognition." Recognition is generally free and goes a long way towards making employees feel **appreciated**. In fact, recognition is often more effective than even monetary rewards.

3. **Discipline:** You need to <u>privately</u> and calmly correct poor performance, using a progressive process that leads inexorably to either improved performance or removal from the job.

Correcting Poor Performance

Disciplining or correcting a poorly performing employee, or even someone who is doing a pretty good job but is not working up to their potential, does not need to be a frightening or traumatic event for either the manager or the employee. To discipline effectively and legally you need to follow some specific steps:

1. **Set goals and expectations first.** If the employee does not have a clearly agreed upon goal plan you have no right to discipline the employee.

2. **Provide regular feedback.** If you have noticed poor performance or bad behavior over a period of time and have not discussed it, you have no right to discipline the employee.

3. **Use a three step discipline process.**

The three step discipline process explained

Step 1: Problem solving. Assuming you did a professional job on Points 1 and 2 above, you have a responsibility to point out both good and bad behaviors and results to the employee. The first conversation proceeds as follows:

1. Remind the employee of the fact that you have agreed together to achieve certain expectations;
2. Tell the employee what you saw and the consequences of that observation;
3. Be quiet;
4. Probe to see if there is something going on in the work environment interfering with the employee's ability to perform;
5. Agree on steps for corrective action;
6. Agree on a date to follow up.

One question managers ask me during performance management workshops is, "How long should I allow before I follow up again?" There is no set answer, such as 30 days. You have to allow sufficient time to observe whether the employee really improved, but not so much time that further non-performance drags down the organization.

Here is an example of the first discussion.

Manager: "Bill, I want to talk to you about filling out work orders completely. When we met in January we agreed that you were going to always fill the work orders out completely. But yesterday I noticed that you sent in two work orders with the materials specification missing, and one did not have all the measurements. When the guys down in the fab got your paperwork they had to waste 45 minutes figuring out the missing details before they could get to work. That delay made us miss the production target for the day. Is something keeping you from getting the orders filled out completely?"

Employee: "Things get hectic and I just do not have time to fill out the orders and still see all the patients!"

Manager: "So as you see it, the paperwork takes too much time to fill out when things are really busy."

Employee: "Yes, that's right"

Manager: "Bill, I can understand that things get hectic, but I need you to keep your agreement on those work orders. The people in the fab are depending on you!" [now problem solve together] "What if you came in early and filled out some of the boiler plate in advance, like your name, employee number, the names of the patients on the schedule for the day, etc. Then you only have to write in the final details when you send in the order."

Employee: "Well, I guess I could do that"

Manager: "We really need to get complete work orders. Can we agree to make that change?"

Employee: "OK, that would work."

Manager: "Great, I'll meet with you on the first of next month to see how it went."

During the first conversation to correct a problem, you **assume the best**. Assume that the employee is trying his best and is either not clear on the expectation or some-thing in the work environment is getting in the way of his performance. Perhaps he needs some training, resources, or help. Ninety percent of the time this will be the case, and you will never have to talk about it again. When he starts performing better, you have the fun of recognizing his accomplishment!

While it is important to have a verbal conversation, you must follow it up in writing to the employee and/or to the file, to document that you have followed fair and sound practices in case of future legal questions. If you handle the conversation and the documentation professionally, you have no need to worry about legal fallout.

Step 2: Follow up. For the second conversation you go through the same steps as above, but with one difference. If the issues preventing good performance are a matter of the job conditions, you problem solve as before. Barriers to good performance due to job conditions are less likely to be the case in the second meeting, since you have already dealt with those issues in the first meeting. If there is still a lack of performance after the first meeting, the cause is usually a lack of willingness or ability on the part of the employee to do what is required to get good results.

This time you insist that the employee provide you a written plan about what he is going to do to correct the problem. At this meeting you emphasize that you expect him to improve, and further shortfall will result in his removal from the job. You will not necessarily terminate his employment, but you may have to change his responsibilities to better match his skills if he cannot get good results in his current position. Having earned the right to manage by setting conditions and providing feedback, you can now hold the employee accountable for his part. Remember, before you come down on an employee for poor performance, you must make sure you did your job as the manager.

If the employee does not have the ability to do the job, but has a good attitude and has made best efforts to perform, the proper response is to **re-align** the employee into a different position which more closely matches her abilities. While sometimes that is not possible, you should try to do that whenever you can.

If the employee is not performing because he is unwilling to do the things he needs to do to get the results, he is choosing, by his behavior, to leave the organization. Your best move, in that instance, is to **separate** the employee from the organization and assist him in finding a more suitable employer outside your company.

Before you separate an employee from the organization, be sure you review all the process steps, conversation, and documentation with your supervisor and legal counsel. If you have followed the steps, you should be in a strong position to separate the employee.

Step 3: End the process. The process never goes beyond three meetings. At the third meeting, the employee has either improved to the point where he is performing acceptably, or he has not.

If the employee is performing acceptably, you have the privilege of recognizing his achievement. Congratulations. You have effectively coached an employee to better performance. This is something to feel really good about, and should always be your motive and objective when working with employees.

If by the third meeting the employee is still not performing, you either re-align or separate the employee. Period. No second, third, or fourth chances.

If you have followed the process and documented everything, you have every right to take action. In fact you have a **responsibility** as a manager to not continually tolerate a non-performing employee.

Allowing the situation to continue hurts the organization in terms of business performance, and it sends a message to the other employees that poor performance is "OK".

Remember, you are not doing the non-performing employee any favors by allowing him to keep on failing. The best thing for him is to find a more suitable job and/or employer where he can succeed and enjoy his work.

Remember, if the employee is talented, has a good attitude, has really made the effort, but just does not have the **ability** to do that particular job even after training and coaching, you re-align him **if possible** to another job within your organization. Of course, there may not be another position available for that employee, but you make the effort on his behalf. But if the employee is simply **unwilling** to do what it takes to get the job done, you separate him from the company.

Ideas: Providing Consequences

Double Check: Have I earned the right to manage? - Have I set clear expectations? - Am I providing feedback?	
My regular feedback process	
Rewards I can use	

Recognition I can use	
Corrections I need to make	
My 3 step discipline process	

Chapter 6

Creating a System

An excellent performance management system is nothing more than a series of conversations placed on a calendar. In the following example, I have included a system used by a health care supplier in New York. Your system may look different, and that's okay, as long as the basic elements are there. An effective system must include agreements around objectives and standards for performance, and some way of providing regular feedback on results against those targets. You might find quarterly review too frequent. You might find quarterly review too infrequent. The point is to pick a cycle that fits with how you do

> *An excellent performance management system is nothing more than a series of conversations placed on a calendar.*

business. The "right" timing between reviews will be based on how long it takes to measure results in your business. Ask yourself how long it takes to see the

results of a change in your business approach. The
answer to that question will tell you the cycle that fits
your business.

The Performance Management Cycle: Example

Step 1: Organization Goal Plans & Budgets

Step 8: Contract Renewals

Step 2: Unit Goal Plans & Budgets

Step 7: Annual Salary Reviews

Step 3: Manager Goal Plans

Step 6: Annual Performance Reviews

Step 4: Individual Performer Goal Plans

Step 5: Quarterly Performance Reviews

<u>The basic pattern for managing performance is as</u>
<u>follows:</u>

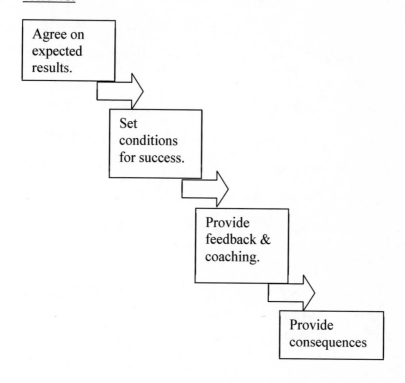

Let's examine each part of the process:

Agree on Expected Results.

Every employee should have a goal plan. This goal plan describes what the employee is expected to accomplish in the coming twelve months and how success will be measured. This plan can also include objectives for improvement in professional skills and behaviors.

The goal plan should be completed before the beginning of each year.

The goal plan for each employee is an **agreement** between the manager and the employee as to what will be accomplished and to what standard of performance it will be accomplished. As such, the conversation around objectives must be a dialog.

Your objective as the manager is to encourage the employee to take **ownership** and responsibility for the goal plan, not to view it as "something management told me I have to do." To gain that sense of ownership, it is important to take certain steps.

1. **Lead by example.** You must have a goal plan yourself, and you must share that plan with your employees as an example to follow. You cannot

hold employees accountable for standards which you are not willing to hold yourself to.

2. **Ask for input.** Talk together with an employee about the basic categories of expectations for the position. Then let the employee come back to you with his proposal for what the goals and standards ought to be. Then discuss and come to agreement on the final version. Often employees will set higher goals for themselves than management would! Clearly, **you have the prerogative to make the final "call" on the objectives**, but the more involved the employee is in getting to the end point the more committed he will be to delivering on the plan.

3. **Confirm agreement.** When you have the conversation, use phrases such as, "So Bill, then we agree that our target for 2002 productivity will be 78%. Is that right?" Unless both your head and the employee's head are nodding "yes" you do not have agreement.

4. **Put it in writing.** Make sure the goal plan is in writing. You will refer back to it often during the year as you talk about how the employee is doing against her plan.

5. **Write "SMART" goal statements.** Specific, Measurable, Achievable, Relevant, and Time Sensitive.

Here are some examples of SMART goal statements:

- "Wendy will make sure all the patient files are kept in order and current (within 1 day). The first review will be March 1st. Other reviews will be quarterly through the rest of the year."
- "Bill will achieve $425,000 in sales volume for the core product line by 12/31/2002."
- "Carla will complete goal plans for all her employees by 2/1/2002."

- "Janet will have quarterly performance reviews with each employee, with summaries sent to headquarters within two weeks after the end of the quarter."

Feedback and Coaching.

Once you have agreed upon a goal plan with your employee, you have the right to hold him **accountable** for the plan. You also have the responsibility to provide regular **feedback** to the employee, both positive and negative, as to how he is doing. Unless you are totally unethical, you will not "save up" dirty laundry on your employee for months and then "drop the bomb" on him at your convenience.

You also have the responsibility to teach and coach the employee to do her best. It is not enough to simply tell her, "I expect you to improve." You have a responsibility to help her improve. To be a good "coach" you need to do certain things well.

1. **Establish your coaching role up front.** A coach is someone who has **permission** to give feedback on performance. When the coach and player on an athletic team have a good understanding up front about their roles, the player expects the coach to give feedback, and will listen when it is given.

2. **Balance feedback.** Make it a regular habit of "catching people in the act of **doing things right**." You should do about 80% positive to 20% negative. If you give lots of positive feedback you will have no problem bringing up the corrections when needed. Why? Because the employee will trust that you have his best interests at heart. Earn that trust so that you can give correction when needed.

3. **Give behavioral feedback.** The goal of providing feedback is to give the employee something specific that she can either keep doing or improve. Transmitting hearsay, gossip, and generalizations will only frustrate the performer.

66

"Judgmental" feedback, such as "great" or "poor", is useless for both of you.

The employee needs to understand **what he specifically did** or did not do that caused a certain outcome. Then the employee can modify his behavior to get better results.

For Example:

- "When you fill out the work orders completely [behavior & standard], that makes Tom's job in the shop much more efficient, resulting in better productivity for the company [impact of behavior]. I really appreciate how you have made sure to do that!"

- "When you speak abruptly [behavior] to the people in the branch offices, it makes them feel that you do not respect them, so

they are not motivated to help you get
what you need [impact of behavior]."

4. **Give regular feedback.** Employees need to
    know right away if they are doing something
    wrong. Timely feedback does not necessarily
    mean in the moment, but you need to pick the
    right time and place to give feedback. It does
    mean "timely", which means within a day or two
    of the event that you observed.

Use the right time and place.

If the employee is under the gun to get product out the
door and feeling stressed out, wait until a less tense time
to give the feedback. Ideally you can set up a regular
meeting where you talk about these things one-on-one.
Never give negative feedback in front of others. There is
a difference between "correction" and "humiliation".

Your goal is to help the employee improve, not to demoralize another human being.

Ideas: My Performance Management System

Setting objectives	
Creating commitment	
Performance appraisal	

Linking to compensation	
My calendar of events	

Chapter 7

Deploying a System

Once you design a system, you need to make it stick. Most organizations, even those with world class systems designed by industry experts, do not fully **deploy** their policies. Yet without full compliance to the system, it quickly falls apart.

Even worse than lack of compliance, some organizations have **surface compliance**. In other words, managers and employees go through the motions of the performance management activities, but do not take them seriously. They fill out the forms, have performance appraisal meetings, and update annual goal plans, but do not actually alter their **behavior** as a result of the process.

To the human resource organization it may appear that the company has a vibrant performance management system, but in fact what they have is elegant **window dressing**.

Why do organizations resist using a performance management system when the benefits are so compelling? More importantly, how can you overcome that resistance so that people actually embrace the process? Here are six major areas to focus on:

1. **Make it a priority.** Have you ever walked into an organization and had people tell you they were not incredibly busy? The demands of day-to-day operations keep managers fully engaged in handling customer demands. In fact, handling day-to-day operations often produces greater personal rewards and satisfaction than the work of management does. The manager gets kudos, accolades, and attention from above when she gets the product out the door. When she takes time to manage employees, no one notices. Is it any wonder that she spends her time getting product out the door?

2. **Keep it simple.** If the system becomes a "feed the beast" exercise, people will avoid it like the plague. Lengthy forms with detailed instructions head right

for the trash bin. Keep forms simple and limited to one or two pages. The forms used to document goal-setting and performance reviews ought to be nothing more than **user-friendly tools** to make the manager's job easier, and never an end unto themselves. The point of a good form is to help the manager and employee have a good conversation and to document the key points.

Today, most companies are moving toward on-line forms. Again, keep them simple. Complex java-scripted web pages, prone to crashes, will turn people away in droves.

If you "force" employees to use the system "or else", with an arbitrary deadline to comply, you will get meaningless surface compliance.

3. **Train the managers.** If managers are not thoroughly trained to use the system, they will often avoid using it rather than risk making a mistake. You must ensure that managers know the rationale for the system, and how to use the system.

4. **Walk the talk.** The primary reason that performance management does not get used is the behavior of the top management. Put simply, if the senior management uses the system with their staff, the mindset will cascade to all levels. If the senior manager gives lip service to or ignores the principles, then others will follow suit. People do what they think is important, and usually that will be what they think senior management cares about.

5. **Be courageous.** Talking openly with employees about expectations and job performance can be a scary business. Frankly, most people are taught from an early age to avoid confrontation. Very few managers are skilled at how to talk about job performance.

Many supervisors would rather transfer a problem employee to another department than take responsibility for correcting that individual's performance. Effective dialog between employees and managers builds clarity, agreements, and trust. Avoidance of issues breeds frustration and distrust

While avoidance may seem appealing to a busy manager with customers lighting up every phone line, employee performance issues will only grow worse if left unattended. Eventually, the manager will be forced to take action when the problem becomes a crisis.

Additionally, managers just do not know how to have effective conversations with employees about tough issues. If they feel unskilled and awkward, they will avoid the conversations. You must provide training, practice, and on-going coaching on how to skillfully confront poor performance.

6. **Emphasize values, not just "skills".** Skills training, without an ethical foundation of effective management principles, does nothing but spread manipulative techniques. If a manager has not done her homework and earned the right to manage, equipping her with confrontation skills will turn her

into an artful tyrant. So please, whenever you do "skills" training, be sure to combine it with foundational principles of sound, ethical management.

Parting Comments.

Are you ready to create a great place to work? You, the manager, are the single most important factor in a positive work environment. If you commit to developing a sound

> *You, the manager, are the single most important factor in a positive work environment.*

performance management system and to honing your skills to talk with people about performance, you will be well on your way to making a real difference. I thank you for taking the challenge, but more importantly, your organization, and your employees, will thank you for doing the right thing.

Recommended Reading List

Gebelein, Susan; Stevens, Lisa A.; Skube Carol J.; Lee, David G. *Successful Manager's Handbook*, Personnel Decisions International, 2000.

Bolton, Robert, *People Skills*, New York, Simon and Schuster, 1979.

Lebow, Rob. *A Journey into the Heroic Environment, A Personal Guide to Creating a Work Environment Built on Shared Values*, Prima Publishing, 1997.

Block, Peter. *Stewardship*, San Francisco, Berrett-Koehler Publishers, Inc., 1996.

About the Author – Gene C. Mage

Syndicated Business Columnist & Speaker

 Prior to founding Soaring Oaks Consulting Incorporated, Gene C. Mage served for twelve years in management at Corning Incorporated, including: International Market Development, International Education, and Business Research and Analysis.

Gene led Corning's internal consulting department providing services to ten operating divisions around the world. Among his accomplishments, he researched and launched Cranberry Visions cookware, which reached $38.0 million of sales in its first year. He opened Corning's Consumer Products sales office in Tokyo, Japan, and deployed management development for Corning operations in the UK, Japan, France, Germany, and Brazil.

Gene's company has provided services to a variety of companies including Corning Incorporated, The Buffalo News, Gannett, Creative Orthotics & Prosthetics, Inc., and Corning Community College.

Gene has published over seventy articles, and writes the syndicated weekly business column *Making it Work.*

Making it Work™ Keynotes & Seminars

Call to book National Speakers Association member Gene C. Mage for engaging and informative programs targeted to your event theme and objectives. **1-866-290-1404**

MEMBER

NATIONAL
SPEAKERS
ASSOCIATION

Keynote Topics Include:

Creating the Culture of Trust

Discover the three high-integrity leadership actions that can restore trust in a jaded marketplace. Learn to create a high-trust work environment that makes and keeps promises to employees, customers, and investors.

Creating the High-Performance Workplace

Consistent and flexible. Organized, but creative. Dependable, yet fun. Sound like a great place to work? Master these paradoxes and you will build an energizing work environment that is both fun and profitable. This highly practical program shows the way.

Making it Work™ Training Workshops

Managing for High Performance – A lively, energizing workshop that equips managers with essential tools for a building a high-trust, high-accountability work environment. Available in half-day, one-day, and two-day formats.

Customer Relationship Skills – A fast paced one-day workshop that equips front line customer service personnel with the tools to delight the customer the first time and every time.

All training workshops are customized and delivered on-site by experienced corporate trainers who make learning come alive.

Choose from a wide range of topics including *Time Management, Reader-Friendly Writing for Business*, and *Sailing through Change*. **1-866-290-1404**

Customized Consulting

Gene C. Mage and his network of associates provide **customized solutions** to organizations wishing to create world class management practices in the areas of organizational performance and marketing strategy. **For additional information call 1-866-290-1404 or visit www.makingitwork.com**

How to Order Copies of
Managing for High Performance

Phone: Call Toll Free (866) 290-1404

8:30 – 5:00 EST Monday - Friday

24/7 voice system

Website: www.makingitwork.com

For secure on-line ordering

Mail: 459 Belwood Drive,

Horseheads, NY 14845

Fax: (607) 795-9799

Use faxable order form on page 85 or 87

Volume Pricing Discounts:

Quantity	Price Each
1-99	$9.95
100 – 499	$8.95
500 – 4999	$7.95
5000 +	Call for discount.

Shipping and Handling = $4.00 + 6% of total

FAXABLE ORDER FORM

Making it Work™
Call 1.866.290.1404
Or 607.795.9797
Monday through Friday 8:30 a.m. to 5:00 p.m. EST
FAX: 607.795.9799 Online: www.makingitwork.com

Description	Quantity	X Unit Price =	Total
Managing for High Performance			
		Product Total	
		Shipping & Handling* ($4.00 + 6% of total above)	
		Subtotal	
		NYS Only Sales Tax (7%)	
		TOTAL (U.S. Dollars Only)	

BILLING INFORMATION:

❏ *My order is over $250. Please invoice*

Charge your order:
❏ Mastercard
❏ Visa
❏ American Express

Credit Card Account Number:

_____

Expiration Date:
_____/_____
  mo.   year

Print Name:

_____

Cardholder Signature:

_____

❏ Check or
  Money Order enclosed
  Payable to: Making it Work

Prices effective July 1, 2002 are subject to change without notice.

*Shipping & Handling Charges Orders are shipped ground delivery 7-10 days. For faster delivery, please call.

SHIP TO:

Name_____
Title_____
Organization_____
Street Address_____
City_____State_____Zip_____
Phone (____) _____ext_____
Fax (____) _____
E-mail_____

BILL TO: (If different than SHIP TO)

Name_____
Title_____
Organization_____
Street Address_____
City_____State_____Zip_____
Phone (____) _____ext_____
Fax (____) _____
E-mail_____

FAXABLE ORDER FORM

Making it Work™
Call 1.866.290.1404
Or 607.795.9797
Monday through Friday 8:30 a.m. to 5:00 p.m. EST
FAX: 607.795.9799 Online: www.makingitwork.com

Description	Quantity	X Unit Price =	Total
Managing for High Performance			
		Product Total	
		Shipping & Handling* ($4.00 + 6% of total above)	
		Subtotal	
		NYS Only Sales Tax (7%)	
		TOTAL (U.S. Dollars Only)	

BILLING INFORMATION:

❑ *My order is over $250. Please invoice*

Charge your order:
❑ Mastercard
❑ Visa
❑ American Express

Credit Card Account Number:

_____

Expiration Date:
____/_____
mo.   year

Print Name:

_____

Cardholder Signature:

_____

❑ Check or
Money Order enclosed
Payable to: Making it Work

Prices effective July 1, 2002 are subject to change without notice.

*Shipping & Handling Charges Orders are shipped ground delivery 7-10 days. For faster delivery, please call.

SHIP TO:

Name_____

Title_____

Organization_____

Street Address_____

City_____State_____Zip_____

Phone (____) _____ext_____

Fax (____) _____

E-mail_____

BILL TO: (If different than SHIP TO)

Name_____

Title_____

Organization_____

Street Address_____

City_____State_____Zip_____

Phone (____) _____ext_____

Fax (____) _____

E-mail_____

Share the joy!

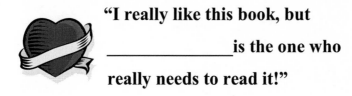

"I really like this book, but _____ is the one who really needs to read it!"

Yes, we know. Every business has that "special someone" who could use the information in *Managing for High Performance*. But how can you send him or her the book without being too "forward" about the matter?

Making it Work will send a copy of this book to that "special someone" on your list. Just log onto **www.makingitwork.com** and click on the "Share the Joy" link for details on a special offer.

In a few days the book will be sent confidentially. It will magically appear on their desk, marked with the special inscription, *"Someone you know wants you to read this book."*

"Share the joy" and help create a better work environment!

Notes